BOOKS BY STEPHEN SPENDER

The Generous Days
Selected Poems
Collected Poems
The Edge of Being
Poems of Dedication
Ruins and Visions
Poems
The Still Centre
Trial of a Judge

THE
GENEROUS
DAYS

RANDOM HOUSE

NEW YORK

THE
GENEROUS
DAYS

STEPHEN
SPENDER

To Matthew, Maro and Saskia
con amore

CONTENTS

IF IT WERE NOT

If it were not for that
Lean executioner, who stands
Ever beyond a door
With axe raised in both hands —

All my days here would be
One day — the same — the drops
Of light edgeless in light
That no circumference stops.

Mountain, star and flower
Single with my seeing
Would — gone from sight — draw back again
Each to its separate being.

Nor would I hoard against
The obliterating desert
Their petals of the crystal snow
Glittering on the heart.

My hand would never stir
To follow into stone
Hair the wind outlines on sky
A moment, and then gone.

What gives edge to remembering
Is death. It's that shows, curled,
Within each falling moment
An Antony, a world.

She came into the garden
And, walking through deep flowers, held up
Our child who, smiling down at her,
Clung to her throat, a cup.

Clocks notch such instances
On time: no time to keep
Beyond the eye's delight
The loss that makes it weep.

I chisel memories
Within a shadowy room,
Transmuting gleams of light to ships
Launched into a tomb.

LOST DAYS (to John Lehmann)

Then, when an hour was twenty hours, he lay
Drowned under grass. He watched the carrier ant,
With mandibles as trolley, push in front
Wax-yellow specks across the parched cracked clay.

A tall sun made the stems down there transparent.
Moving, he saw the speedwell's sky blue eye
Start up next to his own, a chink of sky
Stamped deep through the tarpaulin of a tent.

He pressed his mouth against the rooted ground.
Held in his arms, he felt the earth spin round.

THE CHALK BLUE BUTTERFLY

The Chalk Blue (clinging to
A harebell stem, where it loops
Its curving wirefine neck
From which there hangs the flowerbell
Shaken by the wind that shakes
Too, the butterfly)—
Opens now, now shuts, its wings,
Opening, shutting, on a hinge
Sprung at touch of sun or shadow.
   Open, the sunned wings mirror
Minute, double, all the sky.
   Shut, the ghostly underwing
Is cloud-opaque, bordered by
Copper spots embossed
By a pigmy hammering.

   I look and look, as though my eyes
Could hold the Chalk Blue in a vice,
Waiting for some other witness
— That child's blue gaze, miraculous.
But today I am alone.

BOY, CAT, CANARY

Our whistling son called his canary Hector.
"Why?" I asked. "Because I had always about me
More of Hector with his glittering helmet than
Achilles with his triple-thewed shield." He let Hector
Out of his cage, fly up to the ceiling, perch on his chair, hop
Onto his table where the sword lay bright among books
While he sat in his yellow jersey, doing his homework.
Once, hearing a shout, I entered his room, saw what carnage:
The Siamese cat had worked his tigerish scene.
Hector lay on the floor of his door-open cage
Wings still fluttering, flattened against the sand.
Parallel, horizontal, on the rug, the boy lay
Mouth biting against it, fists hammering boards.
"Tomorrow, let him forget," I prayed. "Let him not see
What I see in this room of miniature Iliad —
The golden whistling howled down by the dark."

A FATHER IN TIME OF WAR

I

On a winter night I took her to the hospital.
Lying in bed, she clasped my hand
In her two hands. I watched the smile
Float on her pain-torn happy face —
Light stretched on the surface of a well
At the bottom of which, hidden from sight,
Curled a minute human phantom.

II

Next morning, I went to hospital
On a bus that drove through streets
Unwinding back to the First Day.
A solitary street cleaner
Hosed water over hopeless rubble.
In front of her charred and splintered door
A woman scrubbed
A doorstep whiter than her hair.
A ladder lifted up into the air
Arms that bore a minute human phantom.

III

Now we watch him lying in the grass
In the garden. His eyes
See branches sway. Birds fly forward
Against the backwards-flying clouds.
Brushing yellow flowers, green leaves, his eyes
Pout like his mouth across her breast:
Voluptuous wondering, drinking in
The dizzy spinning tilting upside-
down flags of the world new born.

CHILD FALLING ASLEEP IN TIME
OF WAR

Smooth the sheet. Then kiss her forehead —
Bone shell the ocean dreams inside.
Dark is voyage. This bed, her boat
Drawn up on the incoming tide
One word, "goodnight", will thrust afloat.

Sleeping, my child seems this calm air
That she smiles through. Her breathing is,
Moment to moment, star to star,
Measure of the measureless
Nature dreaming under war.

ALMOND TREE BY A BOMBED CHURCH
(for Henry Moore)

Jewel-winged almond tree,
Alighting here on bended knee —
To the shattered street you bring
Annunciation of Spring —

Where, before, an angel was
That wrestled in the leaded glass,
Now, risen from the fallen window,
Leaves and burning petals glow.

Resurrected from the dust
Of bricks and rubble, blood and rust,
Luminous new life appears
On leaf and petal, trembling spears.

V. W. (1941)

That woman who, entering a room,
Stood, staring round at all, with rays
From her wild eyes, till people there
— And books, pictures, furniture —
Became transformed within her gaze
To rocks, fish, wrecks, Armada treasure —
Gold lit green on the sea floor —

Filled her dress with heavy stones
Then lay down in a shallow brook
Where a wave, like casing glass,
Curves over her shattered face,
And clothes — torn pages of her book —
Mad mind as cold and silent as the stones.

MEIN KIND KAM HEIM (after Stefan George)

My boy came home
The seawind still curves through his hair —
  His step still weighs
Fears withstood and young lust for adventure.

The saltbrine spray
Still brands the bronze bloom of his cheek:
  Rind quickly ripened
In foreign suns bewildering haze and flame.

His glance is grave
Already with some secret hidden from me
  And lightly veiled
Since from his Spring he to our winter came.

So sudden burst
This burgeoning that almost shy I watched
  And forbade mine
His mouth that chose another mouth as kiss.

My arm surrounds
Him who unmoved from mine for other worlds
  Blossoms and grows —
My one my own endlessly far from me.

SLEEPLESS

Awake alone in the house
I heard a voice
— Ambiguous —
With nothing nice.

Perhaps knocking windows?
A board loose in the floor?
A gap where a draught blows
Under the door?

Repairs needed? Bills?
Is it owls hooting — pay! —
Or it might be the walls
Crumbling away

Reminding — "You, too,
Disintegrate
With the plaster — but you
At a faster rate."

Or it might be that friend once
I shut outside
Sink or swim — well, he sank —
In my sleep cried

"Let me in! Let me in!",
Tapping at the pane.
Him I imagine,
Twenty years in the rain.

THE GENEROUS DAYS

I

His are the generous days that balance
Soul and body. Should he hear the trumpet
Shout justice from a sky of ice
— Lightning through the marrow —
At once one with that cause, he'd throw
Himself across some far, sad parapet —
Soul fly up from body's sacrifice,
Immolated in the summons.

II

But his, too, are the days when should he greet
Her who goes walking, looking for a brooch
Under plantains at dusk beside the path,
And sidelong looks at him as though she thought
His glance might hide the gleam she sought —
He would run up to her, and each
Find the lost clasp hid in them both,
Mindless of soul, so their two bodies meet.

III

Body soul — soul body — are his breath
— Or light or shadow cast before his will —
In these, his generous days. They prove
His utmost being simply is to give.
Wholly to die, or wholly, else, to live!
If the cause ask for death, then let it kill.
If the blood ask for life, then let it love.
Giving is all to life or all to death.

IV

After, of course, will come a time not this
When he'll be taken, stripped, strapped to a wheel
That is a world, and has the power to change
The brooch's gold, the trumpet's golden blaze
— The lightning through the blood those generous days —
Into what drives a system, like a fuel.
Then to himself he will seem loathed and strange,
Have thoughts still colder than the thing he is.

ON THE PHOTOGRAPH OF A FRIEND, DEAD

Dead friend, this picture proves there was an instant
That with a place — leaf-dazzling garden — crossed
When — mirror of midday — you sent
Shadow and light from living flesh into
The sensitive dark instrument

That snatched your image for its opposite
And, in a black cell, stood you on your head.
So, on the film, when I developed it,
Black showed white, where you had shadow, white
Black, where smiling up, your eyes were sunlit.

To me, under my hand, in the Dark Room
Laid in a bath of chemicals, your ghost
Emerged gelatinously from that tomb;
Looking-glass, soot-faced, values all reversed
The shadows brilliant and the lights one gloom.

Reverse of that reverse, your photograph
Now positively scans me with
Your quizzical ironic framed half-laugh.
Your gaze oblique under sun-sculptured lids
Endlessly asks me: "Is this all we have?"

VOICE FROM A SKULL
(Futami-ga-ura, Ise-Shima. *For Peter Watson*)

     I

Here, where the Pacific seems a pond,
Winds like pocket knives have carved out islands
From sandstone, to *netsuke*:

                    Pekingese,
With rampant ruffs and fan-spread claws,
Scratch at coiff'd waves.

                     A pirate junk
Lobs cones from conifers (its mast
That solitary pine trunk staved
With two dead boughs).

                    Porcupine,
Tortoise, dragon, cormorant.

     II

                    Our boat throbs on
Through sea and sky, the seamless bowl
Of solid light in which pearl fishers dive.
It thrusts through scarcely lifting waves;
— Long rollers moving under silk —
A stretching and unstretching surface.
Fisherboats are delicate
As water-boatmen.

                          We land
Where a path skirts the rocks. Twined ropes
Are slung between two boulders to lasso
At dawn the sun, risen for pilgrims.
Following the path, I reach a park
With cliffs hewn into caves embossed
With hieroglyphs . . .

                          In one cave,
A hermit sits. He scrapes a tune
Upon one hair outstretched of his white beard.
His bow's his bone-thin arm.

                    IV
Suddenly I hear your voice,
Inside my skull, peal — like the tongue
Inside a pilgrim's bell — peal out
In those gay mocking tones I knew:

                          "You were
Once my companion on a journey
The far side of the world, the Alps,
Rock-leaded windows of Europe.
You saw fields diamonded as harlequin
Reflected on my laughing eyes, who now
Am dragged under the soil in a net
That tangles smile and eyeballs with
Their visions rainbowed still.

                          But you,
Lacking my eyes through which you looked,
Turn like a shadow round the sunlit dial."

FIFTEEN LINE SONNET IN FOUR PARTS

I

When we talk, I imagine silence
Beyond the intervalling words: a space
Empty of all but ourselves there, face to face,
Away from others, alone in the intense
Light or dark, it would not matter which.

II

But where a room envelopes us, one heart,
Our bodies, locked together, prove apart
Unless we change them back again to speech.

III

Close to you here, looking at you, I see
Beyond your eyes looking back, that second you
Of whom the outward semblance is the image —
The inward being where the name springs true.

IV

Today, left only with a name, I rage,
Willing these lines — willing a name to be
Flesh, on the blank unanswering page.

WHAT LOVE POEMS SAY

In spite of this
Enormity of space —
Total distance total dark between
Lights all ice all fire
Adverse to all of life —

Nevertheless, I wake
This morning to this luck, that you
On a second of a clock
Into a measured space, this room,
Come, as though
Spiralling down a staircase of
Immeasurable light-years —
Here and Now made flesh,
With greeting in your eyes,
Lips smiling, willing to respond,
Hand extended.

It is as though I were
In all the universe the centre
Of a circumference
Surrounding us with lights
That have eyes watchful, benevolent —
Looked on us and concentrated
Their omnipresence in one instance —
You, come with a word.

FOUR SKETCHES FOR
HERBERT READ

INNOCENCE

Farm house, green field. Stone
White in grey eyes.
The innocent gaze
Simplifies forms
To rectangle, circle.
The sun in the skull
Dissolves a world to light.

YOUNG OFFICER

Young officer, leaning
Against a bayonet hedge
Of blackthorn, its white
Blossom, your medals.
Your soldiers graze
Like sheep. You are their shepherd.
Mournful bugles
Engraved those lines
Either side your mouth.

CONFERENCIER

I took a pencil up
Idly at some conference,
Drew the lick of hair
Surround to your face.
The bow tie beneath
Marked a question mark's dot.
In the hall of chairs
Fat platitudes sat.
You stood out like a question.

ANARCHIST

When you died, I was in France.
Supposing you were sad —
Listen. I saw the students
Thread the streets in dance.
Their heels struck fire.
Their hands uprooted pavements.
Their mouths sang the chant
Of a poet's final hour:
Imagination seizes power.

TO W. H. AUDEN ON HIS SIXTIETH BIRTHDAY

You — the young bow-tied near-albino undergraduate
With rooms on Peck Quad (blinds drawn down at midday
To shut the sun out) — read your poems aloud
In so clinical a voice, I thought
You held each word gleaming on forceps
Up to your lamp. Images seemed segments
On slides under the iciest of microscopes
Which showed white edges round dark stains
Of the West collapsing to a farce:
Not to be wept over, since the ruins
Offered the poet a bare-kneed engineer's
Chance of scrambling madly over scrap heaps
To fish out carburettors, sparking plugs,
A sculptured Hell from a cathedral porch,
Scenes from sagas and a water-logged
Lost code. With nicotine-stained fingers
You rigged such junk into new, strange machines.
Two met at dawn (riders against the sky line),
A spy crouched on the floor of a parched cistern,
One with hands that clutched at the wet reeds
Was shot, escaping. Your words lobbed squibs
Into my solemn dream, the young Romantic's
Praying his wound would blossom to a rose
Of blood, vermilion under a gold moon,
Exclaiming — "O!"
                                    Forty years later, now, benevolent
In carpet slippers, you still make devices,
Sitting at table, playing patience,
Grumpily fitting our lives to your game
Whose rules are dogma of objective love.

ONE MORE NEW BOTCHED BEGINNING

Their voices heard, I stumble suddenly
Choking in undergrowth. I'm torn
Mouth pressed against the thorns,
                            remembering
Ten years ago, here in Geneva
I walked with Merlau-Ponty by the lake.
Upon his face, I saw his intellect.
Energy of the sun-interweaving
Waves, electric, danced on him. His eyes
Smiled with their gay logic through
Black coins flung down from leaves.
                            He who
Was Merlau-Ponty that day is no more
Irrevocable than the I that day who was
Beside him — I'm still living!

   Also that summer
My son stayed up the valley in the mountains.
One day I went to see him and he stood
Not seeing me, watching some hens.
Doing so, he was absorbed
In their wire-netted world. He danced
On one leg. Leaning forward, he became
A bird-boy. I am there
Still seeing him. To him
That moment — unselfknowing even then
Is drowned in the oblivious earliness . . .

Such pasts

Are not diminished distances, perspective
Vanishing points, but doors
Burst open suddenly by gusts
That seek to blow the heart out . . .

Today I see

Three undergraduates standing talking in
A college quad. They show each other poems —
Louis MacNeice, Bernard Spencer, and I.
Louis caught cold in the rain, Bernard fell
From a train door.

Their lives are now those poems that were
Pointers to the poems to be their lives.
We read there in the college quad. Each poem
Is still a new beginning. If
They had been finished though they would have died
Before they died. Being alive
Is when each moment's a new start, with past
And future shuffled between fingers
For a new game.

I'm dealing out

My hand to them, one more new botched beginning,
Here, where we still stand talking in the quad.

MATTER OF IDENTITY

Who he was, remained an open question
He asked himself, looking at all those others —
The Strangers, roaring down the street.

Explorer, politician, bemedalled
General, teacher — any of these
He might have been. But he was none.

Impossible though, to avoid the conclusion
That he had certain attributes: for instance,
Parents, birthdays, sex. Calendars

Each year the same day totted up his age.
Also, he was a husband and had children
And fitted in his office, measure to his desk.

Yet he never felt quite certain
Even of certainties: discerned a gap
(Like that between two letters) between statistics

(These he was always writing out on forms)
And his real self. Sometimes he wondered
Whether he had ever been born, or had died . . .

(A blank space dreaming of its asterisks)
    *   *   *   *   *   *
Sometimes he had the sensation
Of being in a library, and reading a history

And coming to a chapter left unwritten
That blazed with nothing . . . nothing except him
. . . Nothing but his great name and his great deeds.

TO BECOME A DUMB THING

Sunset.
At the harbour mouth headlands of agate.
Lamps stab needles into the pleating water.
Fishermen stand or sit, at quayside, in boats, mending nets.
One, without a word, gets up, goes over to another, helps
him, goes back.
*   *   *   *   *   *   *
We sit at our café table by the waves.
Talk Paris New York London places we shall/shan't visit.
The temples! The bullring! The blood!
Red hot corpses shed into the Ganges!
Gossip! Friends! Enemies!
Playing over worn scenes on a worn reel.
*   *   *   *   *   *   *
Six fishermen wade out. Clamber onto a boat. One advances
to the end of the jetty to which several boats, with men and
women on them, are tied. He pisses into the sea.
*   *   *   *   *   *   *

Their life is things. Their thoughts are things.
They touch things. The fish nudges against the hook. The
hook pricks the gullet. The line tugs against the horn
hand. The nets balance moon-glittering scales.
*   *   *   *   *   *   *   *   *   *
At day's end the sun, a raging ball, topples them over
one by one. Falling into beds. Flailing arms. Into
one another. Drunk.
*   *   *   *   *   *   *   *   *   *
To be them would mean throwing aside Christian's burden
when he forsook wife and children . . .
to . . .
unwind this coil . . .
crawling on all fours . . .
begging life from beggars . . .
to become a dumb thing.

BAGATELLES

I   AFTER THE INSCRIPTION ON A GREEK STELE OF A
     WOMAN HOLDING HER GRANDCHILD ON HER KNEES

My daughter's dear child here I hold on my lap: so
I used to hold him of old in those days
When with living eyes we both looked on the sun:
Now that he's dead, I still hold him: for I
Am dead too.

II   M.J. (1940)

That running boy with mouth raised up
Hands stretched towards the winning cup
Eyes starting forth: lies on the ground
His victory drained away through a small wound.

III   FOR HUMPHRY HOUSE

When you became a Christian, mocking (not mocking) I said
"Then bless me!" You growled "Kneel!" So I knelt
                down there in the High.
I carry this like an amulet always. You know —
If you watch from bright air under earth where you lie.

IV   SENTENCED

He thought of the blank paper as
Where he should be what he was:
His writing, as the sap that flows
Along the stem into the rose.
Words, straight from the heart, his song
Being from his heart, could not go wrong.
All he had to do was be
His real self blazing through the tree.
So he wrote, without pretence
His truth.
                    That was his youth.
                                        Each sentence
Stands written in his book.
                                    Indeed,
His sentence there for all to read.

V   DESCARTES

Lightning, enlightening, turns
Midnight to one flash of white.
Startled, people, steeples, hens
Shudder into sight.
Dogs bark. Cocks crow. Descartes
Writes in chalk across black sky:
I think therefore I
Am. Words a sponge deletes.
Black blackness blackens.

VI   MOSQUITO

Filigree mosquito
Afloat in black air
Anchors above my head,
Tinsel trumpet blowing
In the tomb of my ear.
Angel of Fra Angelico
Awakening me, dead,
To such thoughts as make
Midnight Judgement Day.

VII   MOON

Moon, I don't believe in you!
Yet now I almost do
Seeing you (above those rectangles
Of windows — triangles
Of roofs — squares of squares —
And through those scimitars
Of silhouetted leaves)
Describe your lucid circle —
Exultant disk buoying up
A map that mocks our Earth.

VIII   PRESENT ABSENCE

You slept so quiet at your end of the room, you seemed
A memory, your absence.
I worked well, rising early, while you dreamed.

I thought your going would only make this difference:
A memory, your presence.
But now I am alone I know a silence
That howls. Here solitude begins.

IX   AFTER TIBULLUS

Absolute passion which I thought I'd shown
These past few days to thee, my sole delight,
Let me no more make boast of, if I've done
Ever one act that caused me greater shame,
Bitterer self-reproach, than that last night:
The offence of leaving thee all night alone,
Through seeking to dissimulate my flame.

X   A POLITICAL GENERATION

When they put pen
To paper, in those times,
They knew their written
Ten lines with five rhymes,
Before the reader had turned
The page over, might have burned.

With such doubts, how could they doubt
Their duty — to write
Poems that put fires out
To keep lights alight?
So, putting first things first,
They did their best to write their worst.

XI   TO MY JAPANESE TRANSLATOR (SHOZO)

My English writing runs into your eyes
Then reappears along your finger tips
And through the brush upon the paper
In characters — to me — snow crystals.

We look into each other's faces:
In mine, your eyes, in yours, mine, opposite.
Midway between us both, our tongues
Change you to me and me to you.

XII   RENAISSANCE HERO

A galaxy of cells composed a system
Where he was, human, in his tower of bones.
The sun rose in his head. The moon ran, full,
Vermilion in the blood along his veins.
His statue stood in marble in his glance.

Body and intellect in him were one.
Raised but his hand, and through the universe
Relations altered between things in space.
Before his step, light opened like a door.
Time took the seal of his intaglio face.

CENTRAL HEATING SYSTEM

I'm woken up
By the central heating system. An engine
Thuds in the cellar. Steam clanks in pipes
With distinct sounds — cymbals banged together.
The snow falls outside
Hushing up the scandal of the dark,
Whitewashing the blackness of the boughs.
But here, in the room, the pipes must make their scene.
Like a long watch dog curled through the whole house,
They bark at the ice-fanged killer
Who leaves no footstep in the night.

(Storrs, Connecticut)

ART STUDENT

With ginger hair dragged over
                            fiery orange face
Blue shirt, red scarf knotted round his neck,
Blue jeans, soft leather Russian boots
Tied round with bands he ties and unties when
His feet are not spread sprawling on two tables —
Yawning, he reads his effort. It's about
A crazy Icarus always falling into
A labyrinth.
                    He says
He only has one subject — death — he don't know why —
And saying so leans back scratching his head
Like a Dickensian coachman.
                       Apologizes
For his bad verse — he's no poet — an art student —
— Paints — sculpts — has to complete a work at once
Or loses faith in it.
                    Anyway, he thinks
Art's finished.
                There's only one thing left
Go to the slaughter house and fetch
A bleeding something-or-other — oxtail, heart,
Bollocks, or best a bullock's pair of lungs,
Then put them in the college exhibition,
On a table or hung up on a wall
Or if they won't allow that, just outside
In the courtyard.

                              (Someone suggests
He put them in a plastic bag. He sneers at that.)

The point is they'll produce some slight sensation —
Shock, indignation, admiration. He bets
Some student will stand looking at them
For hours on end and find them beautiful
Just as he finds any light outside a gallery,
On a junk heap of automobiles, for instance,
More beautiful than sunsets framed inside.
That's all we can do now — send people back
To the real thing — the stinking corpse.

ACKNOWLEDGEMENTS AND NOTE

Acknowledgements for leave to reprint poems are due to the
editors of: The Listener, The London Magazine,
The New York Review of Books, The Observer, The Poem of the
Month Club, Poetry (Chicago), Poetry (London), Queen,
The Sunday Times and The Times Literary Supplement.
Acknowledgements are also due to Mr. Eric Walter White
and the Poetry Book Society.

I am also grateful to my friend Mr. David Godine of
Brookline, Massachusetts, for printing, very beautifully,
a handset edition of ten of these poems, under the same
general title *The Generous Days*. There were 250 copies of
this edition which is out of print.

Note: I have reprinted *One More New Botched Beginning* from
my *Selected Poems* (Faber, London, and Random House, New York)
because it seemed to sum up the mood of elegiac reminiscence
of the poems that precede it in this volume.

ABOUT THE AUTHOR

STEPHEN SPENDER was born in London in 1909 and was educated at Oxford University. Together with W. H. Auden, Louis MacNiece and C. Day Lewis, he helped to forge a new consciousness and style in English poetry. He is presently a Professor of English at University College, London.

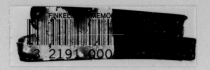

	DATE	